Moments

with

Jesus

Coloring Book

This book belongs to:

Moments with Jesus: Coloring Book
~ Rik Feeney

ISBN: 978-1-935683-28-5 (Paperback)

Richardson Publishing, Inc.
PO Box 162115
Altamonte Springs, FL 32716
www.RickFeeney.com
407-529-8539
usabookcoach@gmail.com

Disclaimer:
This book is a work of creative art design using a historical religious figure. Every attempt has been made to be respectful and appropriate in each illustration depicted. The purpose of this coloring book is to provide a vehicle for conversation between children and adults and between adults and religious mentors. In addition, it is hoped this coloring book will help relieve depression and anxiety. The pictures contained herein do not promote or suggest any particular aspect of Christianity. This coloring book is intended to help educate, inspire, challenge, and create a few moments of relaxation every day using designs drawn from the life of Jesus Christ.

Permissions:
Vecteezy.com Pro License

Artist Name: _____

Date: _____

Title: _____

Dedicated to: _____

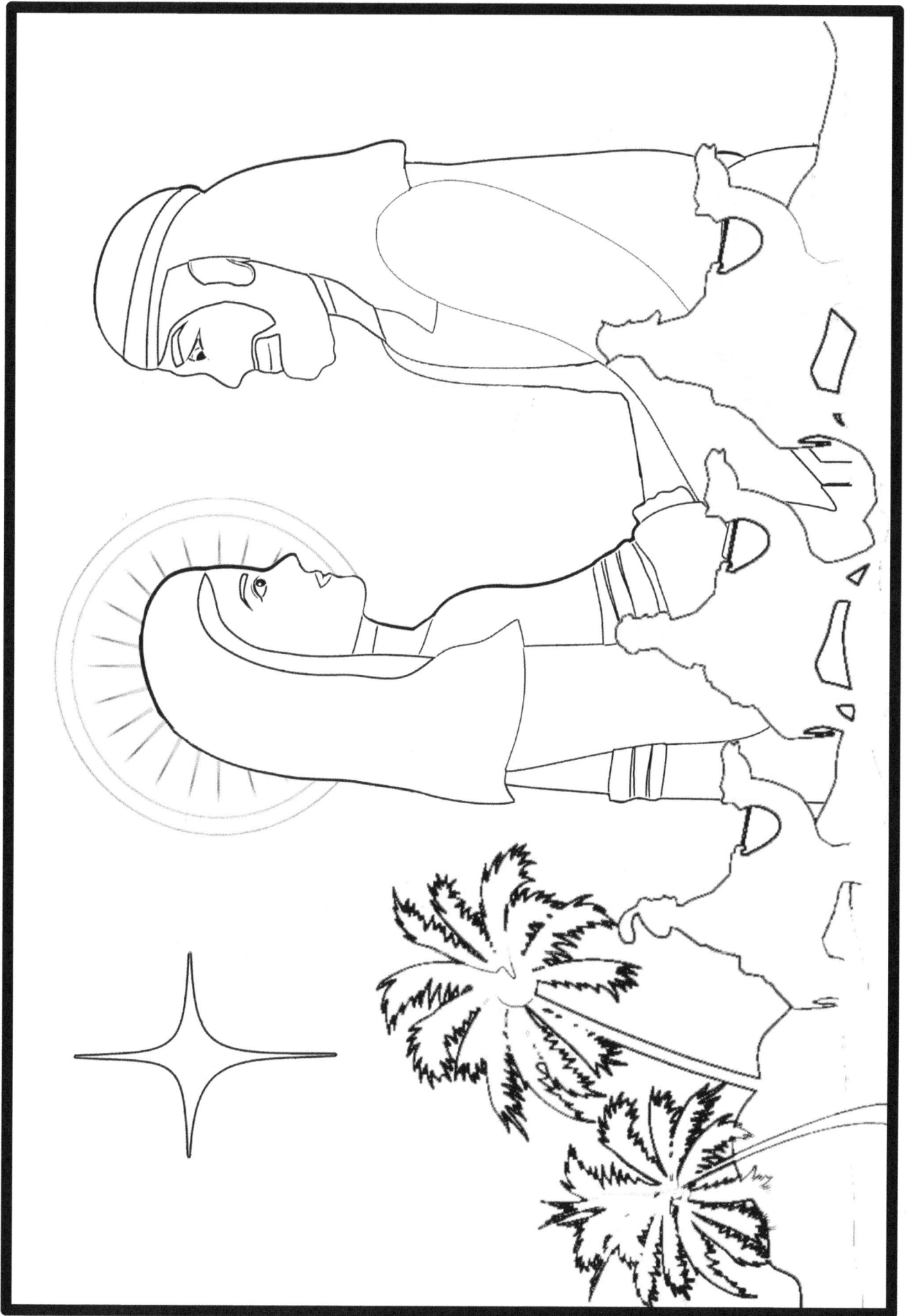

Artist Name: _____

Date: _____

Title: _____

Dedicated to: _____

Artist Name:_____

Date:_____

Title:_____

Dedicated to:_____

Artist Name: _____

Date: _____

Title: _____

Dedicated to: _____

Artist Name:

Date:

Title:

Dedicated to:

Artist Name:_____

Date:_____

Title:_____

Dedicated to:_____

Artist Name: _____

Date: _____

Title: _____

Dedicated to: _____

Artist Name: _____

Date: _____

Title: _____

Dedicated to: _____

Artist Name: _____

Date: _____

Title: _____

Dedicated to: _____

Artist Name: _____

Date: _____

Title: _____

Dedicated to: _____

Artist Name: _____

Date: _____

Title: _____

Dedicated to: _____

Artist Name: _____

Date: _____

Title: _____

Dedicated to: _____

Artist Name:

Date:

Title:

Dedicated to:

Artist Name:_____

Date:_____

Title:_____

Dedicated to:_____

Artist Name:_____

Date:_____

Title:_____

Dedicated to:_____

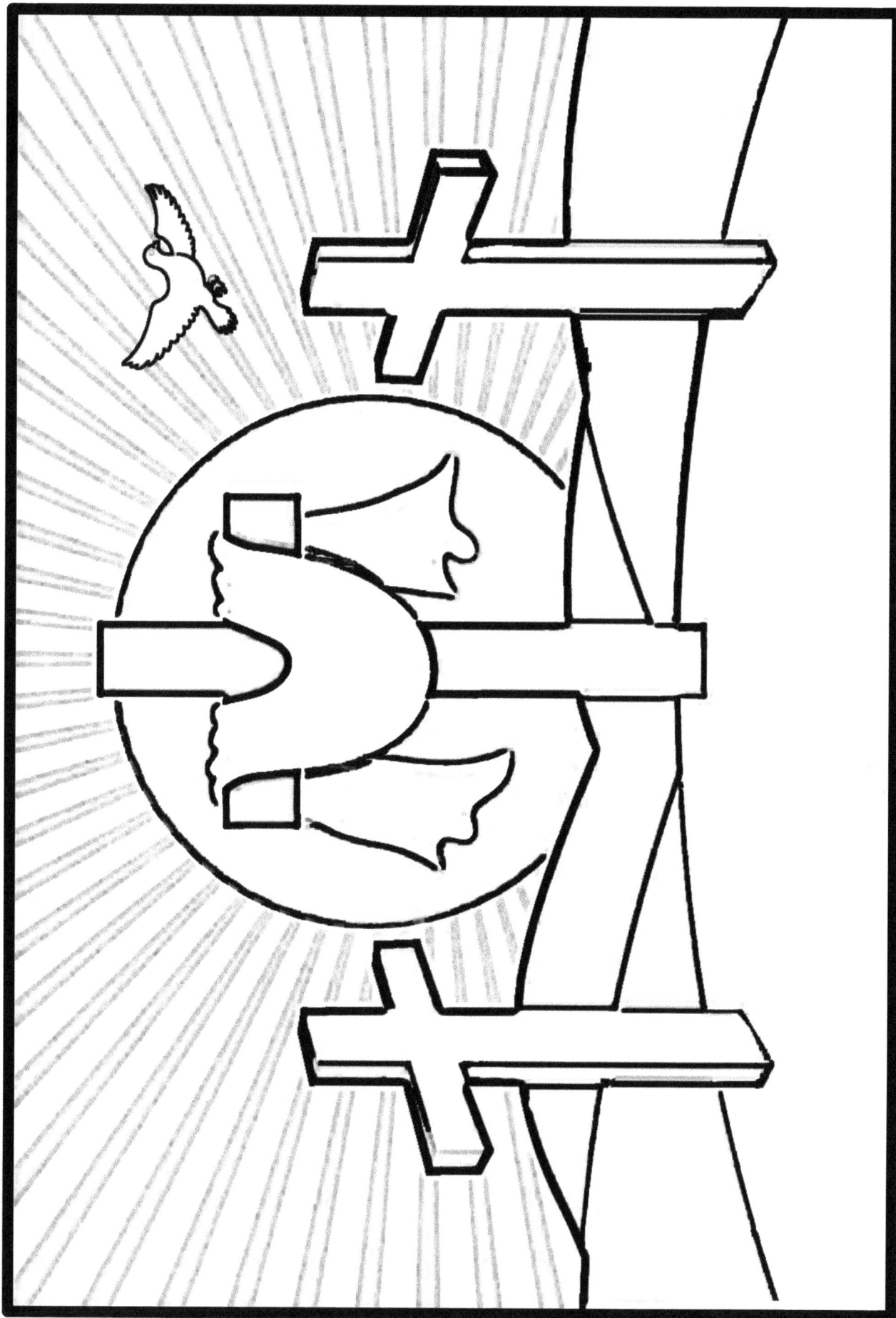

Artist Name: _____

Date: _____

Title: _____

Dedicated to: _____

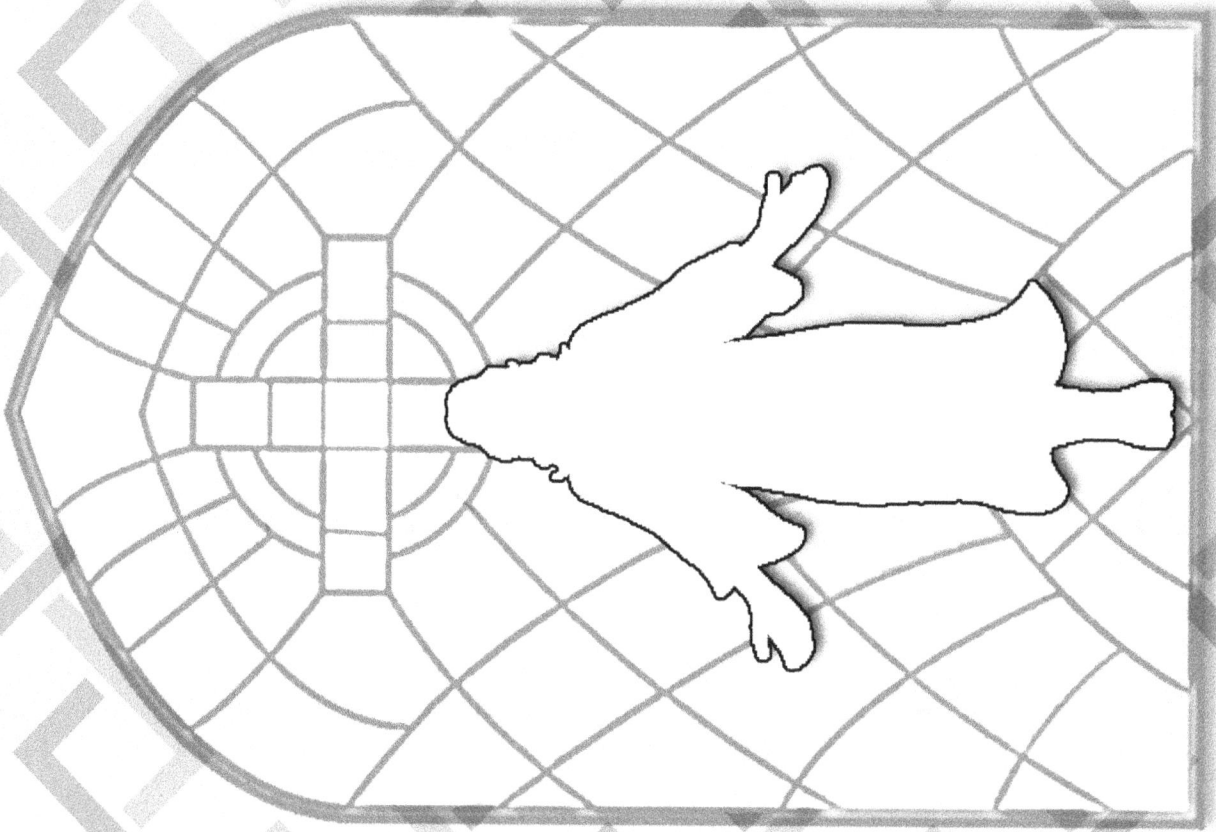

Artist Name: _____

Date: _____

Title: _____

Dedicated to: _____

Artist Name: _____

Date: _____

Title: _____

Dedicated to: _____

Artist Name:_____

Date:_____

Title:_____

Dedicated to:_____

Artist Name: _____

Date: _____

Title: _____

Dedicated to: _____

Artist Name: _____

Date: _____

Title: _____

Dedicated to: _____

Artist Name: _____

Date: _____

Title: _____

Dedicated to: _____

Artist Name: _____

Date: _____

Title: _____

Dedicated to: _____

Artist Name:_____

Date:_____

Title:_____

Dedicated to:_____

Artist Name: _____

Date: _____

Title: _____

Dedicated to: _____

Artist Name:_____

Date:_____

Title:_____

Dedicated to:_____

Artist Name:_____

Date:_____

Title:_____

Dedicated to:_____

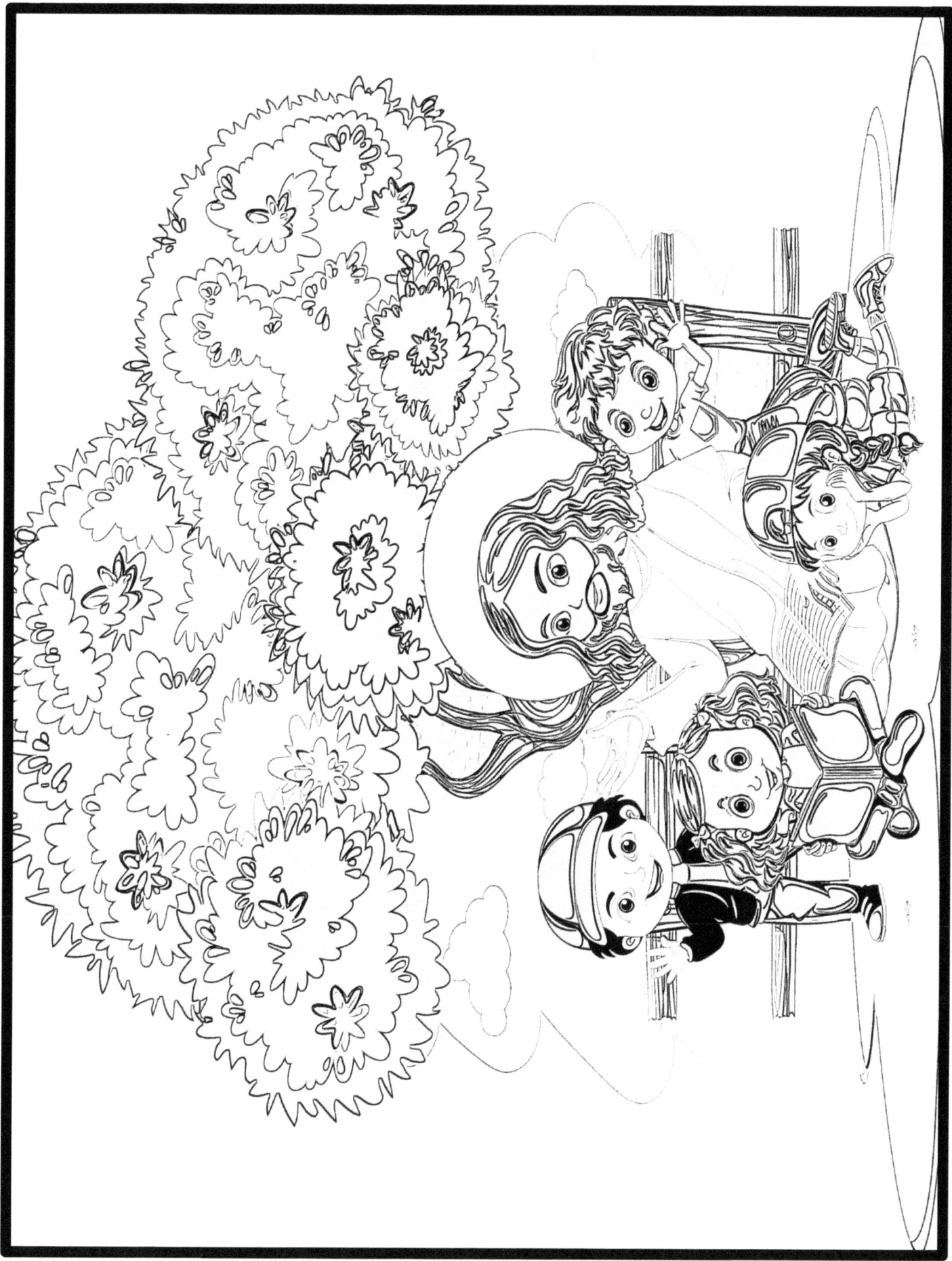

Artist Name: _____

Date: _____

Title: _____

Dedicated to: _____

Artist Name:_____

Date:_____

Title:_____

Dedicated to:_____

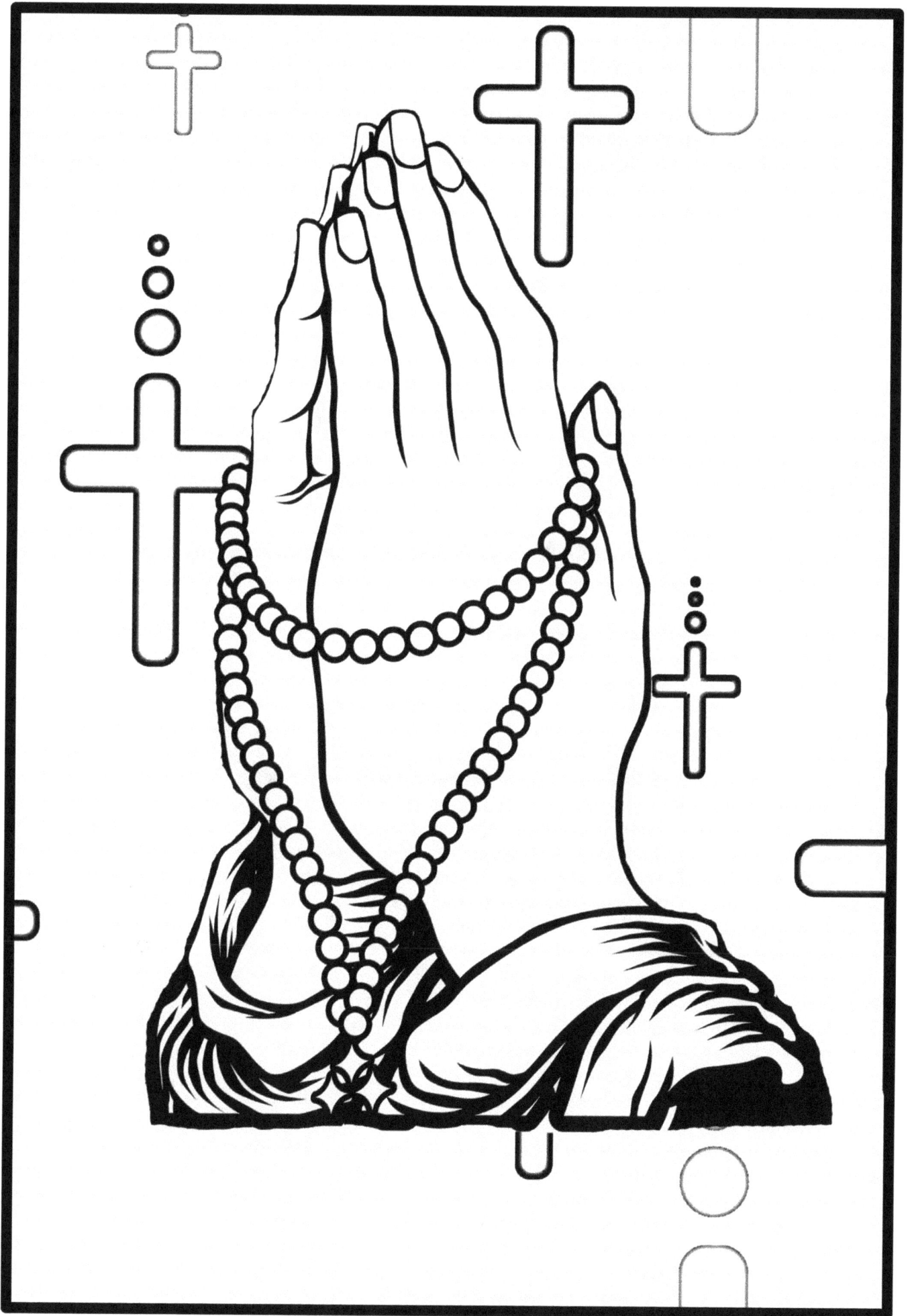

Artist Name:_____

Date:_____

Title:_____

Dedicated to:_____

Dear Artist,

Hope you had fun coloring these pages? Please send me an email and let me know what you thought or, if you would do me the very great favor, and write a review online where you got this coloring book.

Let me know if you have any ideas for additional illustrations or different coloring book themes.

I look forward to hearing from you.

All the best,

Rik Feeney
usabookcoach@gmail.com
www.RickFeeney.com